I0190072

GOD'S LISTENING

Promises of God

BY ANITA WAMBLE

Copyright © 2016 by Anita Wamble
Published by Refined Concepts, Fort Washington, MD

All rights reserved. No portion of this publication may be reproduced, stored in a retrieval system or transmitted in any form by any means— except for brief quotations in printed reviews—without the prior written permission of the author.

ISBN-13: 978-0692758694
ISBN-10: 0692758690

Printed and bound in the U.S.A.

www.anitawambleministries.com
www.refinedconcepts.net

It only seems correct to dedicate this book to Elohim, the only wise, all knowing and ever existing One, who inspired everything in this book.

God and God alone deserves all honor, glory and praise!

A PRAYER BOOK LIKE NO OTHER

I love to pray! It's probably because of my upbringing. My mother and grandmothers were what the old saints would call "pray warriors." People from all over the country would call them and ask my mother or grandmothers to pray for them or a loved one. People said my mother and grandmothers could, "get a prayer through."

Well the truth is, we can all "get a prayer through" because God is always listening to our prayers. In Mark 11:24 Jesus said, "Therefore I tell you, whatever you ask for in prayer, believe that you have received it, and it will be yours."

In order for God to give us what we need, we have to pray. If we're not praying, there's nothing for God to listen to; which means we don't receive what we need or want because we haven't prayed.

If God is listening, why aren't we praying?

Some people believe that you have to have a degree in the King James Version of the Bible in order to pray. Other people think they can't pray because of the things they are doing or have done in the past. Still others simple don't make the time to pray. All of these and so many more excuses we use for not praying are just that, excuses.

The prayer book and journal that go along with this Promises of God booklet, were written to help the reader move into a greater relationship with God through prayer.

1. The pray book and journal were designed to:
2. Encourage the reader to pray
3. Encourage the reader to journal
4. Encourage the readers to log their prayer requests and when the prayers are answered.

Remind the reader about the promises of God. How are these objectives accomplished?

This booklet is a companion pieces to the God's Listening

prayer book and journal. In the prayer book are over 100 prayers designed to help the reader focus on their spiritual growth, their family and self-care, the reader's immediate community and the international community.

These prayers cover important elements in our lives like forgiveness, spiritual growth, increasing our moral character and faith in God. There are even prayers to help us during some of the most difficult times of our lives, the holiday seasons.

In the prayer book are of words of encouragement from me. Sometimes, you just need to know that someone has been where you are, has traveled the road you're on and with God's protection, grace and mercy, they made it through the rough times, which means, and so can you.

In the prayer journal there are pages to log your prayer request and to note when your prayers are answered. There are scriptures and quotes from notable people to help you focus on the truth of God's word and your ability to operate in greatness.

Use this booklet when you're journaling, as an easy reference, to help remind you of God's promises to you.

My challenge to you is to use this booklet, the book of prayers

and the companion journal for 40 days and watch how prayer can change your life.

Min. Anita Wamble

CONTENTS

Anger

For His anger lasts only a moment, but His favor last a lifetime; weeping may remain for a night, but rejoicing comes in the morning. *Psalms 30:5*

My dear brothers, take note of this: Everyone should be quick to listen, slow to speak and slow to become angry, for man's anger does not bring about the righteous life that God desires. *James 1: 19—20*

Do not be quickly provoked in your spirit, for anger resides in the lap of fools. *Ecclesiastes 7:9*

A hot-tempered man stirs up dissension, but a patient man calms a quarrel. *Proverbs 15:18*

Proverbs 14:17 ● Colossians 3:21 ● Proverbs 25:21—22
Psalms 145:8 ● Romans 12:19—21 ● Colossians 3:8

Belief

I tell you the truth; he who believes has everlasting life. *John 6:47*

Whoever believes in Him is not condemned, but whoever does not believe stands condemned already because he has not believed in the name of God's one and only Son. *John 3:18*

I have come into the world as a light, so that no one who believes in Me should stay in darkness. *John 12:46*

John 3:16 ● Acts 10:43 ● Romans 9:33 ● John 1:12
John 3:36 ● I Peter 2:6 ● Acts 16:31

Children

For I will pour water on the thirsty land, the streams on the dry ground; I will pour out my Spirit on your offspring. *Isaiah 44:33*

The promise is for you and your children and for all who are far off—for all whom the Lord our God will call. *Acts 2:39*

Proverbs 17:6 ● *Mark 10:14—16* ● *Acts 16:31*
Psalms 127:3—5

by Anita Wamble

Comfort

Though I walk in the midst of trouble, You preserve my life; You stretch out Your hand against the anger of my foes, with Your right hand You save me. *Psalm 138:7*

For in Him you have been enriched in every way—in all your speaking and in all your knowledge. *I Corinthians 1:5*

The Lord is a refuge for the oppressed, a stronghold in times of trouble. *Psalm 9:9*

Wait for the Lord; be strong and take heart and wait for the Lord. *Psalm 27:14*

I have told you these things, so that in Me you may have peace. In this world you will have trouble. But take heart! I have overcome the world. *John 16:33*

Psalm 18:2 ● *Nahum 1:7* ● *Lamentations 3:31—33*
II Corinthians 1:5 ● *Matthew 11:28*

Contentment

Keep your lives free from the love of money and be content with what you have because God has said, "Never will I leave you; never will I forsake you." *Hebrews 13:5*

But godliness with contentment is great gain. *I Timothy 6:6*

Proverbs 17:22 ● *Proverbs 15:15* ● *Proverbs 14:30*
Proverbs 23: 17—18

Courage

Trust in the Lord, and do good; dwell in the land and enjoy safe pasture. *Psalm 37:3*

I can do all things through Christ who strengthens me. *Philippians 4: 13*

Psalm 27:14 ● Psalm 37:28 ● II King 6:16
Isaiah 40:29

Enemies

For the Lord your God is one who goes with you to fight for you against your enemies to give you victory. *Deuteronomy 20:4*

And will not God bring about justice for His chosen ones, who cry out to Him day and night? Will He keep putting them off? I tell you, He will see that they get justice, and quickly. *Luke 18:7 —8a*

Psalm 37:40 ● Job 8:22 ● Deuteronomy 28:7
Job 5:20 ● Psalm 60:23 ● Isaiah 54:17
Psalm 27: 5—6

Faith

You are all sons of God through faith in Christ Jesus. *Galatians 3:26*

For we walk by faith, not by sight. *II Corinthians 5:7*

...so that Christ may dwell in your hearts through faith. And I pray that you, being rooted and established in love, may have power together with all the saints, to grasp how wide and long and high and deep is the love of Christ, and to know this love that that surpasses knowledge—that you may be filled to the measure of all the fullness of God. *Ephesians 3:17—19*

...let us fix our eyes on Jesus, the author and perfecter of our faith... *Hebrews 12:1—2*

Hebrews 11:1 ● *Hebrews 11:6* ● *James 1:5—6*
Colossians 2:6—7 ● *Ephesians 2:8*
II Timothy 3:14—15 ● *I Corinthians 16:13*
Galatians 5:22—23 ● *Galatians 2:20* ● *Mark 11:22—23*

Fear

For I am the Lord your God who takes hold of your right hand and says to you, Do not fear; I will help you. *Isaiah 41:13*

...but whoever listens to Me will live in safety and be at ease, without fear of harm. *Proverbs 1:33*

Have no fear of sudden disaster or of the ruin that overtakes the wicked, for the Lord will be your confidence and will keep your foot from being snared. *Proverbs 3:25—26*

For God has not given us a spirit of fear, but of power and of love and of self-discipline. *II Timothy 1:7*

God is our refuge and strength, an ever-present help in trouble. *Psalm 46:1*

*Mark 4:40 ● Matthew 10:28 ● Isaiah 14:3 ● Proverbs 3:24
I Peter 3:12—14 ● Isaiah 54:14 ● Romans 8:15 ● Hebrews 13:6
Proverbs 29:25 ● Psalm 91:4—6 ● Isaiah 54:4 ● Isaiah 43:2
John 14:27 ● Psalm 23:4—5 ● Psalm 27:1—3
Romans 8:37—39*

by Anita Wamble

Forgiveness

And when you stand praying, if you hold anything against anyone, forgive him, so that your Father in Heaven may forgive you your sins. *Mark 25—26*

Therefore, if you are offering your gift at the altar and there remember that your brother has something against you, leave your gift there in front of the altar. First go and be reconciled to your brother; then come and offer your gift. *Matthew 5:23—25*

On the contrary: If your enemy is hungry, feed him; if he is thirsty, give him something to drink. In doing this, you will heap burning coals on his head. *Romans 12:20*

Matthew 5:44—45 • Matthew 6:14 • Luke 6:35—38
Proverbs 20:22

Guilt

But if we walk in the light, as He is in the light, we have fellowship with one another, and the blood of Jesus, His Son, purifies us from all sin. *I John 1:7*

If we confess our sins, He is faithful and just and will forgive us our sins and purify us from all unrighteousness. *I John 1:9*

Therefore, if anyone is in Christ, he is a new creation; the old has gone, the new has come! *II Corinthians 5:17*

Isaiah 55:7 ● II Chronicles 30:9 ● Psalm 103:12 ● I John 3:20
Hebrews 8:12 ● Jeremiah 31:34 ● Jeremiah 33:8
I John 2:12 ● Isaiah 43:25

Help in Trouble

Those who sow in tears will reap with songs of joy. He, who goes out weeping carrying seed to sow, will return with songs of joy, carrying sheaves with him. *Psalm 126:5—6*

The Lord is a refuge for the oppressed, a stronghold in times of trouble. *Psalm 9:9*

Surely God does not reject a blameless man or strengthen the hands of evildoers. He will fill your mouth with laughter and your lips with shouts of joy. *Job 8:20—21*

Psalm 37:39 ● Psalm 146:8 ● Nahum 1:7 ● Psalm 37:24
Psalm 32:7 ● Psalm 71:20 ● Psalm 42:11 ● Psalm 73:26
Psalm 91:10—11 ● Psalm 31:23 ● Psalm 68:13 ● Job 5:19
Psalm 22:24 ● Psalm 138:7 ● Psalm 34:19
Lamentations 3:31—33 ● Psalm 18:2 ● Micah 7:8 –9
John 16:33

Hope

Why are you downcast, O my soul? Why so disturbed within me? Put your hope in God, for I will yet praise Him, my Savior and my God. *Psalm 42:11*

Therefore, prepare your minds for action; be self-controlled; set your hope fully on the grace to be given you when Jesus Christ is revealed. *I Peter 1:13*

Everyone who has this hope in Him purifies himself, just as He is pure. *I John 3:3*

I Peter 1:21 ● *Proverbs 14:32* ● *Colossians 1:5*
Colossians 1:27 ● *Psalm 31:24* ● *Psalm 71:5*

Joy

You will go out in joy and be led forth in peace; the mountains and hills will burst into song before you, and all the trees of the field will clap their hands. *Isaiah 55:12*

I have told you this so that My joy may be in you and that your joy may be complete. *John 15:11*

...yet I will rejoice in the Lord, I will be joyful in God my Savior. *Habakkuk 3:18*

Nehemiah 8:10 ● Isaiah 41:16 ● Psalm 63:5 ● Psalm 68:3
John 16:22 ● Job 22:26 ● Psalm 33:21 ● I Peter 1:8
Isaiah 61:10 ● Psalm 89:15—16 ● Psalm 118:15 ● Psalm 4:7
Psalm 126:5—6 ● Psalm 97:11—12

God's Love

The Lord your God is with you; He is mighty to save. He will take great delight in you, He will quiet you with His love, He will rejoice over you with singing. *Zephaniah 3:17*

We love because He first loved us. *I John 4:19*

May our Lord Jesus Christ Himself and God our Father, who loved us and by His grace gave us eternal encouragement and good hope, encourage your hearts and strengthen you in every good deed and word. *II Thessalonians 2:16—17*

John 16:27 ● John 17:23, 26 ● I John 4:10, 16
Ephesians 2:4—7 ● Jeremiah 32:41 ● Jeremiah 31:3
John 3:16 ● Deuteronomy 7:13 ● Psalm 146:8
*Proverbs 15:9 ● Isaiah 62:5_*

God's Protection

You will laugh at destruction and famine, and need not fear the beasts of the Earth. *Job 5:22*

The Lord will keep you from all harm; He will watch over your life. The Lord will watch over your coming and going both now and forevermore. *Psalm 121:7 – 8*

But whoever listens to Me will live in safety and be at ease, without fear of harm. *Proverbs 1:33*

"…No weapon formed against you will prevail, and you will refute every tongue that accuses you. This is the heritage of the servants of the Lord, and this is their vindication from Me," declares the Lord. *Isaiah 54:17*

They will no longer be plundered by the nations, nor will wild animals devour them. They will live in safety, and no one will make them afraid. *Ezekiel 34:28*

Proverbs 18:10 ● *Job 11:18 – 19* ● *Proverbs 3:24*
Deuteronomy 33:12 ● *Psalm 112:7* ● *Psalm 91:9 – 10*
Isaiah 43:1 – 2 ● *Psalm 4:8* ● *Psalm 27:1*

Money

Do not wear yourself out to get rich; have the wisdom to show restraint. Cast but a glance at riches and they are gone, for they will surely sprout wings and fly off to the sky like an eagle. *Proverbs 23:4—5*

But remember the Lord your God, for it is He who gives you the ability to produce wealth, and so confirms His covenant, which He swore to your forefathers, as it is today. *Deuteronomy 8:18*

Whoever trusts in his riches will fall, but the righteous will thrive like a green leaf. *Proverbs 13:7*

Proverbs 22:2 ● *Job 36:15* ● *Proverbs 15:16* ● *Proverbs 28:6*
Psalm 41:1 ● *Proverbs 11:28* ● *Proverbs 11:4* ● *Ezekiel 7:19*
Ecclesiastes 5:10 ● *Proverbs 22:16* ● *Proverbs 28:22*
I Timothy 6:17—19 ● *Ecclesiastes 5:12—14* ● *Job 5:15—16*
Psalm 9:18 ● *Proverbs 23:4—5* ● *Psalm 37:16* ● *James 2:5*
Ecclesiastes 4:6 ● *Psalm 12:5* ● *Proverbs 17:5*
Proverbs 22:22 ● *Proverbs 13:11*

Obedience

Carefully follow the terms of this covenant, so that you may prosper in everything you do. *Deuteronomy 29:9*

Whatever you have learned or received or heard from me, or seen in me—put it into practice. And the God of Peace will be with you. *Philippians 4:9*

If they obey and serve Him, they will spend the rest of their days in prosperity and their years in contentment. *Job 36:11*

Deuteronomy 30:15—16 • Deuteronomy 6:18
Deuteronomy 6:3 • Deuteronomy 7:12 • Deuteronomy 5:29
Matthew 5:19 • Matthew 7:24—25 • Romans 8:28
John 15:10 • John 13:17 • James 1:25 • I John 3:22
Romans 2:13 • John 5:24 • Matthew 12:50 • I John 2:17
Matthew 7:21 • Psalm 106:3 • Hebrew 5:9 • John 8:51

Patience

Let us hold unswervingly to the hope we profess, for He who promised is faithful. *Hebrews 10:23*

Let us not become weary in doing good, for at the proper time we will reap a harvest if we do not give up. *Galatians 6:9*

Consider it pure joy, my brothers, whenever you face trials of many kinds, because you know that the testing of your faith develops perseverance. *James 1:2 –3*

James 5:7—8 ● I Peter 2:20 ● Matthew 24:13 ● Hebrews 6:12 Hebrews 10:36 ● Romans 5:3—4

Peace

...creating praise on the lips of the mourners in Israel. Peace, peace to those far and near, says the Lord, "And I will heal them."*Isaiah 57:19*

Let the peace of Christ rule in your hearts, since as members of one body you were called to peace. And be thankful. *Colossians 3:15*

I will listen to what God the Lord will say; He promises peace to His people, His saints—but let them not return to folly. *Psalm 85:8*

Philippians 4:7 ● Isaiah 32:17 ● Luke 7:50 ● Psalm 37:37
II Thessalonians 3:16 ● John 14:27

Prayer

Then you will call upon Me and come and pray to Me, and I will listen to you. *Jeremiah 29:12*

If you believe, you will receive whatever you ask for in prayer. *Matthew 21:22*

You will pray to Him, and He will hear you... *Job 22:27a*

Salvation

In reply Jesus declared, "I tell you the truth, no one can see the kingdom of God unless he is born again." *John 3:3*

Therefore, if anyone is in Christ, he is a new creation; the old is gone, the new has come! *II Corinthians 5:17*

This is good, and pleases God our Savior, who wants all men to be saved and to come to the knowledge of the truth. *I Timothy 2:3 – 4*

My dear children, I write this to you so that you will not sin. But if anybody does sin we have one who speaks to the Father in our defense: Jesus Christ, the righteous One. His is the atoning sacrifice for our sins, and not only for ours but also for the sins of the whole world. *I John 2:1 – 2*

Colossians 2:13 ● I Timothy 4:9 – 10 ● Romans 5:15
Titus 3:4 – 6 ● John 1:12 – 13

Seeking God

The Lord is with you when you are with Him. If you seek Him He will be found by you, but if you forsake Him, He will forsake you. *II Chronicles 15:2b*

Sow for yourselves righteousness, reap the fruit of unfailing love, and break up your unplowed ground; for it is time to seek the Lord, until He comes and showers righteousness on you. *Hosea 10:12*

And without faith it is impossible to please God, because anyone who comes to him must believe that He exists and that He rewards those who earnestly seek Him. *Hebrews 11:6*

The Lord is good to those whose hope is in Him, to those who seek Him; it is good to wait quietly for the salvation of the Lord. *Lamentations 3:25 – 26*

Acts 17:27 ● *Amos 5:4* ● *Deuteronomy 4:29* ● *Ezra 8 :22*
I Chronicles 28 :9 ● *Job 8 :5 – 6* ● *Psalm 9 :10*
Jeremiah 29 :13

by Anita Wamble

Self-Denial

Then Jesus said to His disciples, "If anyone would come after me, he must deny himself and take up his cross and follow me. For whoever wants to save his life will lose it, but whoever loses his life for Me will find it. What good will it be for a man if he gains the whole world, yet forfeits his soul? Or what can a man give in exchange for his soul?" *Matthew 16:24 – 26*

Those who belong to Christ Jesus have crucified the sinful nature with its passions and desires. *Galatians 5:24*

For the grace of God that brings salvation has appeared to all men. It teaches us to say "No" to ungodliness and worldly passions, and to live self-controlled, upright and godly lives in this present age. *Titus 2:11 – 12*

Romans 8:12 – 13 ● *Matthew 5:39 – 41* ● *Luke 18:29 -30*

Sexual Sin

Because He Himself suffered when He was tempted, He is able to help those who are being tempted. *Hebrews 2:18*

Flee from sexual immorality. All other sins a man commits are outside his body, but he who sins sexually sins against his own body. Do you not know that your body is a temple of the Holy Spirit, who is in you, whom you have received from God? You are not your own; you were bought at a price. Therefore honor God with your body. *I Corinthians 6:18 – 20*

It is God's will that you should be sanctified: that you should avoid sexual immorality; that each of you should learn to control his own body in a way that is holy and honorable, not in passionate lust like the heathen, who do not know God. *I Thessalonians 4:3 – 5*

I Corinthians 6:13 ● *I Corinthians 7:1* ● *I Corinthians 7:8 – 9*
I Corinthians 7:37 ● *I Corinthians 10:13* ● *Revelation 14:4*
Hebrews 13:4 ● *II Peter 2:9*

Sickness

Is there any one of you sick? He should call the elders of the church to pray over him and anoint him with oil in the name of the Lord. And the prayer offered in faith will make the sick person well; the Lord will raise him up. If he has sinned, he will be forgiven. *James 5:14 – 15*

…who forgives all your sins and heals all your diseases… *Psalm 103:3*

Surely He took up our infirmities and carried our sorrows, yet we considered Him stricken by God, smitten by Him, and afflicted. But He was pierced for our transgressions, He was crushed for our iniquities; the punishment that brought us peace was on Him, and by His wounds we are healed. *Isaiah 53:4 – 5*

Matthew 9:28 – 30 ● *Jeremiah 17:14* ● *Matthew 4:23 – 24*
Matthew 9:6 – 7 ● *Jeremiah 30:17* ● *Exodus 23:25*
I Peter 2:24

Success

May He give you the desire of your heart and make all your plans succeed. *Psalm 20:4*

Plans fail for lack of counsel, but with many advisers they succeed. *Proverbs 15:22*

Commit to the Lord whatever you do, and your plans will succeed. *Proverbs 16:3*

There is no wisdom, no insight, no plan that can succeed against the Lord. *Proverbs 21:30*

Genesis 39:23 ● *I Samuel 18:14* ● *Joshua 1:7*
II Chronicles 31:21 ● *Ecclesiastes 10:10*

Word of God

Your statutes are wonderful; therefore I will obey them. The unfolding of Your words gives light; it gives understanding to the simple. *Psalm 119:129 – 130*

Every word of God is flawless; He is a shield to those who take refuge in Him. Do not add to His words, or He will rebuke you and prove you a liar. *Proverbs 30:5 – 6*

"It is written: 'Man does not live on bread alone, but on every word that comes from the mouth of God.'" *Matthew 4:4*

John 1:1 – 4, 14 ● John 17:17 ● Colossians 3:16
II Timothy 2:15 ● Hebrews 4:12 – 13 ● II Peter 1:19 – 21
Revelation 22:18 - 19

ABOUT THE AUTHOR

First Lady Anita Patterson Wamble always wanted to be a teacher, but her mother told her teaching was "beneath her." So she went to the University of California at Berkeley to earn a degree in pharmaceutical research because she wanted to be to develop a chemical compound so people all over the world could have clean water. However, God had another plan.

Despite First Lady Anita's academic pursuits, the hunger to teach never subsided. In 1994, she accepted her call to the ministry. Over the past 19 years, she has taught Sunday school, led Education Ministries at various churches, preached to hundreds in DC, Maryland and Virginia, and led numerous workshops. Her ministry is not a surprise considering she hails from a family that has 23 active ministers in various denominations ranging in offices from local pastors to Bishops.

Several years ago, the Oakland, CA native got frustrated seeing people struggle with simple issues of everyday life. They struggled not because they did not believe in the word of God, but because they didn't know how to apply it to their lives. In 1999 First Lady Anita began writing "It's Still Relative – The Word of God for Today's World." Published in 2005,"It's Still Relative" was written for the every person who has ever read the Bible and walked away saying, "I don't get it."

First Lady Anita is married to Pastor Marvin Wamble and she serves as First Lady Eastern and St. John United Methodist Churches in Lusby, MD. They have two children, Julian and Jenise Wamble, who are the joy of her life. For over 10 years First Lady Anita served as a

Certified Lay Servant and now serves the Lusby Charge as a Certified Lay Minister (CLM). She is the mother of Julian and Jenise Wamble. She is employed by FEMA as a Program Analyst.

First Lady Anita has not abandoned her search for a water purification compound. She continues to teach about the purity of the living water – Jesus Christ.

Her favorite scripture is Ephesians 4:11 – 13: "It was He who gave some to be apostles, some to be prophets, some to be evangelists, and some to be pastors and teachers, to prepare God's people for works of service, so that the body of Christ may be built up until we all reach unity in the faith and in the knowledge of the Son of God and become mature, attaining to the whole measure of the fullness of Christ."

www.ingramcontent.com/pod-product-compliance
Lightning Source LLC
Chambersburg PA
CBHW021149020426
42331CB00005B/972